Cheap Wicked Good!

Volume 2

5-Ingredient Budget-Friendly Recipes for Everyday Meals

Louise Davidson

CONTENTS

BEING ON A BUDGET

Everyone needs to save money sometimes, and cutting down on restaurant meals in favor of budget-friendly home cooking is an excellent way to do it. The great news is that this doesn't mean you have to settle for macaroni and cheese or packaged ramen. The diverse and delicious recipes in this book all contain five ingredients or less, and each meal can be prepared for ten dollars or less for a family of four—in some cases, much less! Nor do you have to sacrifice your health to eat economically. Everything here is far healthier than TV dinners and fast food—things you'll be happy to see your family eating and enjoying. For added convenience, many of these recipes share one or more ingredients, making it easy to shop once and have what you need to make meals throughout the week. All the recipes also have a symbol next to them indicating the cost of the meal:

$ = $5 or less
$$ = $5–$7.50
$$$ = $7.50–$10

When you're pressed for time and on a budget, eating healthy, economical meals can be a major challenge. You're busy; but you have to eat! When you're on your way home from work and people are hungry, it can be very tempting to hit the drive-thru and blow $25 on something that will fill you up quickly. But don't! We can show you how to stretch that $25 to feed your family for two whole days—or longer!

It's well known that hungry people eat to feel full—not necessarily to be healthy or to save money. That's why we don't shop with empty bellies if we can avoid it. However, with these recipes, cooking methods, and shopping tips, we can show you how to plan ahead so your food budget covers your calorie and nutritional needs. The great news is that you'd never guess how inexpensive these meals really are.

For some, the very thought of preparing a healthy meal is an obstacle. So much mess and bother! It's easier to take something out of the freezer and toss it in the microwave. But while the photos on the boxes of frozen meals show lots of colorful vegetables, what's inside usually looks quite a bit different. Besides, they're loaded with preservatives, salt, and sugar, and they always cost more than making your own.

This collection of inexpensive meals has another huge advantage—each recipe has only **five major ingredients!** There won't be a whole lot of peeling and chopping, mixing, or getting out every single container in your kitchen to get a teaspoon of this or a cup of that. **These recipes are simple. They are designed around a few main foods, with only some healthy oils or standard spices to complete the picture.** It's food the way it was meant to be enjoyed.

And time isn't the only thing you'll be saving. When you are using only a few main ingredients, you'll save money as well. You'll be surprised to learn what you can prepare on a budget! We will show you how to combine staple ingredients with a variety of vegetables and spices to create healthy meals that you'll be proud to serve. Our recipes include things like Cinnamon Apple Quinoa, Fish Tacos, Rigatoni with Turkey meatballs, and Pesto Chicken. There is no compromise on quality or flavor—just some planning and a tiny bit of effort.

Tips for Eating Well on a Budget

Plan Ahead!
If you know what you plan to serve for dinner, there is less chance you'll feel frustrated and make an unhealthy choice. You'll also be able to make sure you have what you need on hand, and less of your food will go to waste.

Stock Up—Buy Common Foodstuffs in Bulk
Over time, it pays to build up a stockpile of inexpensive, common ingredients that keep well, like eggs, pasta, flour, dried and canned beans, spices, and so on. This way you'll have more options for what to prepare. Shelling out for a larger bag of oats can save you money in the long run, and you can use them for breakfast cereal, muffins, cookies, and even homemade granola bars.

Shop the Sales!
Eat what's on sale, and stock up if you can. There are some things you know you'll need, and you can save money here. For instance, one can of soup makes two school lunches, and it can be bought for just $0.99 on sale. Also, remember to choose generic brands whenever you can.

Eat Less Meat
We all know we should eat less meat for health reasons, and there's also a big savings to be had here once you know what to make. Instead of serving whole cuts of meat, prepare a soup, casserole, or stir-fry with meat in it. You'll save a bundle, people will be full, and it's better for them!

Beans, seeds, and eggs make excellent meat substitutions, depending on the food category. Try chopped eggs or sunflower seeds on your salad, for instance, or make a stew using lots of vegetables, barley, and beans instead of meat. Beans can be used in stir-fries as well.

Use a Slow Cooker
If you invest in a slow cooker, you can make delicious, hearty meals using less expensive cuts of meat.

Use Leftovers
You've already used the ingredients and spent the time and energy to prepare a meal, so don't let the leftovers go to waste. Here are some easy ways to jazz things up:

- Single portions can be eaten as school or work lunches, or even frozen for later use.
- A bit of salad can go into a flour tortilla with some cheese to make a nice wrap—or add leftover rice to make a burrito!
- One generous serving of leftover casserole can feed four people if you add a can of tomatoes or mixed veggies, some milk, or some broth. Instant soup! Some nice crusty bread on the side rounds it out nicely.

What to Buy

Fruit and Vegetables
Fresh fruits and vegetables are always the best choice; you just have to buy them frequently, in small amounts, so they won't go bad in the fridge. Buy what's in season, and if you can parboil and freeze some, go for it!

Canned vegetables will keep for a long time, but they can be higher in salt. Canned fruits are also handy, but they're often packed in syrup. Choose frozen for things that aren't in season, and buy extra when they're on sale. They keep beautifully and cook up in just moments.

Wholegrain Breads
Bakery wholegrain or rustic breads can bring so much to a meal, even if it's just a breakfast of toast and tea. Find a kind you like, and buy that—you can slice it and keep it frozen if you think you won't finish it while it's still fresh. Wholegrains' complex carbohydrates will take longer for your body to break down, so not only will you feel like you're splurging, you'll stay full longer.

Eggs
If you're looking for an inexpensive and versatile source of protein, the humble egg is just what you need. They're less than fifty cents each, they can be prepared so many different ways, and they keep well, so you can't really buy too many.

Bulk Grains
When you shop for flour, oats, rice, barley, pasta, and quinoa, you'll always save money buying a larger quantity. These healthy grains don't spoil easily, and they'll be very useful in the recipes in this book.

Popcorn kernels can be bought in bulk as well, and popcorn made in an air popper is infinitely better for you than the packaged microwave bags—and also very economical. So save your money—you can always use it to buy some real butter to put on your popcorn!

Pro tip: You can make popcorn in a brown paper bag in the microwave! No oils are required. Just put ⅓ cup in a lunch bag, fold the top closed, and give it a try!

Dried Beans and Lentils

Dried beans need to be soaked overnight and then simmered for a couple of hours, but they're worth it because they're so inexpensive—and they're loaded with fiber and protein that will keep you feeling full. (Did you know you can freeze cooked beans? You can!)

Lentils may be more of an acquired taste, but they cook faster and they're absolutely loaded with nutrition. Curries, soups, and stews all benefit from a handful of these bargain beauties.

Dried beans and lentils will keep for years in a dry, dark cupboard, so don't be afraid to buy them in bulk.

Plain Yogurt

You might not have noticed, but the little cups of sweetened yogurt that you're buying are actually pretty pricey. Instead of these, try getting the bigger container of plain, or natural, yogurt. Kids enjoy making their own creations with fruits of their choosing (or even a spoonful of jam), and you'll save money. If you want the thicker Greek yogurt, try straining the regular kind in some cheesecloth and substituting that.

Herbs and Spices

Bulk stores usually have the best deals on spices, and they carry a wide variety for you to choose from. (Bottles can come from discount stores for pennies apiece.) We suggest you buy smaller quantities of dried herbs and spices because they do lose their flavor over time. With the right amount and combination of spices, your wholesome staples can become something really special, as you'll see in these recipes. If you don't already have them, we suggest these:

- Allspice
- Basil
- Black peppercorns
- Chili powder
- Cinnamon
- Cumin
- Curry
- Dried onion flakes
- Garlic powder
- Nutmeg
- Oregano
- Paprika
- Sage
- Turmeric

Sometimes, fresh herbs can make a huge difference in a dish, and so you will sometimes find them in these recipes. They're well worth the extra few dollars; just be sure not to let them wilt away in the fridge.

Oils and Fats
The oils and fats you use in your cooking are going to have a big effect on the quality of the food, so here we suggest using good quality and cooking with small amounts. Buy in bulk when possible. When you can get butter or a good olive oil on sale, that's worth doing. These will improve the taste and texture of your meals so much that you won't regret the extra bit of expense.

Whole Chickens and Turkeys
When they're on sale, it's hard to beat the value or versatility of a whole chicken. You can cut it up into pieces and fry it. You can slice the bottom and open it up to grill it. You can roast it, of course. Chicken breasts might be convenient, but they're quite

expensive. Legs and wings don't have much meat, and thighs sometimes come with a thick layer of skin that you'll cut off and throw away. You'll get a much better value buying the whole bird.

Once the chicken has been cooked and most of the meat has been eaten, don't discard the carcass! Toss that in a pot and cover it with water. Add vegetable peelings, celery, garlic, and a bay leaf, and let it simmer. You can make a big pot of homemade chicken stock using things you would otherwise have just thrown away.

What to Skip

Fruit Juices
Fruit juices contribute mainly sugars and empty calories to our diets, and the cost can really add up—especially if you live in a state that charges a recycling fee for the containers. Make a habit of drinking water instead, or water with a bit of frozen fruit in it for flavor.

Individually Packaged Snacks
As cute as the characters on the package might be, the crackers or cookies in that little single-serving packet for your child are the same as (or inferior to) the ones you buy in a larger box or bag. These little treats add up to more money and less nutrition for your kids, so phase them out. You can make cookies or cracker-cheese-lunchmeat trays at home for less money, and homemade granola bars are so easy. Preparing these things at home takes more time, but you'll save money and you'll be in charge of the ingredients.

BREAKFAST RECIPES

Spinach Scrambled Eggs

Serves 2 | Prep. time 5 minutes | Cooking time 2 minutes | $

Ingredients
2 teaspoons olive oil
4 large eggs
3–4 cups baby spinach
Kosher salt and ground black pepper to taste
2–4 tablespoons Parmesan cheese, grated
Red pepper flakes (crushed) to taste

Directions
1. Crack the eggs into a mixing bowl; whisk well. Season with black pepper and salt to taste.
2. Add the oil to a skillet or saucepan and heat it over medium heat.
3. Add the spinach and stir-cook for 1–2 minutes until wilted.
4. Add the egg mixture and stir-cook until the eggs are cooked well.
5. Mix in the cheese.
6. Serve warm with some red pepper flakes on top.

Nutrition (per serving)
Calories 226, fat 16g, carbs 3g, protein 17g, sodium 171mg

Ham Red Pepper Muffins

Serves 8 | Prep. time 10 minutes | Cooking time 20 minutes | $

Ingredients
2 tablespoons water
½ pound cooked ham, crumbled
8 eggs
1 cup red bell pepper, seeded and chopped
Salt and ground black pepper to taste
Melted butter (to grease)

Directions
1. Preheat the oven to 350°F or 175°C. Grease 8 muffin tins with melted butter.
2. Crack the eggs into a mixing bowl. Add the water, salt, and black pepper; combine well.
3. Add the ham and red bell pepper; combine well.
4. Transfer the mixture to the muffin cups evenly.
5. Bake for about 18–20 minutes and serve warm.

Nutrition (per serving)
Calories 114, fat 7g, carbs 3g, protein 11g, sodium 428mg

Creamy Scrambled Eggs

Serves 4 | Prep. time 5 minutes | Cooking time 12 minutes | $

Ingredients
8 eggs
2 tablespoons olive oil
1 large onion, finely cut
2 tablespoons sour cream
2 tablespoons parsley, finely cut (to serve)

Directions
1. Crack the eggs into a bowl.
2. Add the oil to a skillet or saucepan and heat it over medium heat.
3. Add the onion and stir-cook to sauté for about 5–7 minutes, or until softened.
4. Add the eggs and stir-cook for 1–2 minutes.
5. Add the sour cream and stir-cook until cooked well.
6. Stir in the parsley and serve warm.

Nutrition (per serving)
Calories 227, fat 16g, carbs 7g, protein 13g, sodium 147mg

Banana Vanilla Pancakes

Serves 4–5 | Prep. time 5 minutes | Cooking time 12 minutes | $

Ingredients
2 cups almond milk or whole milk
2 tablespoons raw sugar
3 cups all-purpose flour
2 ripe bananas, peeled and mashed
½ teaspoon vanilla extract
Cooking oil

Directions
1. Combine all the ingredients in a blender or food processor.
2. Blend until smooth.
3. Add the oil to a skillet or saucepan and heat it over medium heat.
4. Add ⅓ cup of the mixture and cook for 2–4 minutes per side until evenly brown.
5. Repeat the process with the remaining batter and serve the pancakes warm.

Nutrition (per serving)
Calories 346, fat 4g, carbs 23g, protein 14g, sodium 106mg

Apple Walnut Oatmeal

Serves 4 | Prep. time 5–8 minutes | Cooking time 15 minutes | $$

Ingredients
¼ cup brown sugar
1 quart water
2 medium apples, peeled and cored
1 tablespoon butter
2 cups old-fashioned rolled oats
½ teaspoon salt
½ tablespoon cinnamon
½ cup walnuts, chopped

Directions
1. Slice the apples into small pieces.
2. To a skillet or saucepan, add the butter and heat it over medium heat.
3. Add the apple pieces and stir-cook for 4–5 minutes.
4. Stir in the brown sugar and water. Boil the mixture and add the oats, salt, and cinnamon.
5. Turn heat to low and cook for 4–5 minutes or until the oats are cooked well.
6. Serve warm with the walnuts on top.

Nutrition (per serving)
Calories 371, fat 16g, carbs 46g, protein 8g, sodium 326mg

Feta Morning Toast

Serves 4 | Prep. time 5 minutes | Cooking time 5 minutes | $

Ingredients
2 tablespoons dill, finely chopped
2 eggs, whisked
4 slices whole wheat or white bread
1½ cups feta cheese, crumbled
1 tomato, sliced

Directions
1. Preheat the oven to 350°F or 175°C.
2. To a mixing bowl, add the eggs, feta cheese and dill. Combine well.
3. Place the bread slices on a baking sheet and spoon the cheese mixture evenly over them.
4. Toast in the oven for 5–6 minutes or until the cheese turns golden.
5. Top with the tomato slices and serve.

Nutrition (per serving)
Calories 264, fat 14g, carbs 17g, protein 14g, sodium 746mg

Mushroom Cheddar Omelet

Serves 2 | Prep. time 5 minutes | Cooking time 5–6 minutes | $

Ingredients
6 medium eggs
½ white onion, peeled and chopped
6 mushrooms, chopped
2 ounces cheddar cheese, shredded
Black pepper and salt to taste
Vegetable oil (to fry)

Directions
1. Break the eggs into a bowl, season with salt and black pepper to taste, and whisk thoroughly.
2. To a frying saucepan, add the oil and heat it over medium heat.
3. Add the egg mixture and spread evenly.
4. Cook for 2 minutes or until the egg mixture begin to firm.
5. Place the onion and mushrooms on top and sprinkle with cheese.
6. Cook until the edges are light brown, then fold one half of omelet onto the other half.
7. Cook for 2 minutes or until golden brown.
8. Slice and serve warm.

Nutrition (per serving)
Calories 344, fat 21g, carbs 9g, protein 27g, sodium 368mg

Walnut Banana Smoothie

Serves 2–3 | Prep. time 5 minutes | Cooking time 0 minutes | $

Ingredients
2 bananas, peeled and sliced
2 cups whole milk, warm
4–5 walnuts, chopped
4–5 almonds, chopped
1 tablespoon honey
Ice cubes (optional)

Directions
1. Add the milk to a blender or food processor.
2. Add the remaining ingredients and ice cubes if desired.
3. Blend until smooth and serve the smoothie in tall glasses.

Nutrition (per serving)
Calories 546, fat 11g, carbs 42g, protein 8g, sodium 116mg

HEARTY SOUPS

Chicken Pasta Soup

Serves 4 | Prep. time 5 minutes | Cooking time 30 minutes | $$

Ingredients
2 medium carrots, peeled and chopped
1 quart low-sodium chicken broth
1 tablespoon olive oil
1 small onion, peeled and finely chopped
1 large (6-ounce) boneless, skinless chicken breast
½ cup dried orzo
Black pepper and salt to taste

Directions
1. Add the oil to a skillet or saucepan and heat it over medium heat.
2. Add the onions and carrots and stir-cook to sauté for about 4–5 minutes or until softened.
3. Add the broth and chicken breast.
4. Reduce the heat to low, cover with a lid, and simmer the mixture for 15 minutes or until cooked through.
5. Remove the chicken breast; slice and set aside.
6. Add the orzo to the broth mixture; cook for 8–10 minutes or until tender.
7. Return the chicken. Season with black pepper and salt to taste. Serve warm.

Nutrition (per serving)
Calories 216, fat 6g, carbs 21g, protein 16g, sodium 328mg

Bacon Potato Soup

Serves 6 | Prep. time 5 minutes | Cooking time 30 minutes | $$

Ingredients
1 medium yellow onion, peeled and diced
5 medium russet potatoes, peeled and cubed
2 tablespoons butter
1 quart low-sodium chicken broth
½ cup heavy cream
Salt and black pepper
Bacon, cooked and crumbled (to garnish)

Directions
1. To a skillet or saucepan, add the butter and heat it over high heat.
2. Add the onion and stir-cook to sauté for about 5 minutes or until softened.
3. Add the chicken broth and potatoes.
4. Reduce the heat to medium-low and simmer the mixture. Cover it with a lid and cook for 20–22 minutes, until the potatoes are soft.
5. Add the cream and stir gently.
6. Blend the soup mixture in a blender until creamy and smooth.
7. Return the soup mixture to the pot. Season with black pepper and salt to taste.
8. Serve warm with crumbled bacon on top.

Nutrition (per serving)
Calories 365, fat 12g, carbs 46g, protein 10 g, sodium 217mg

Broccoli Cheese & Cream Soup

Serves 4 | Prep. time 5 minutes | Cooking time 20 minutes | $$

Ingredients
1 cup heavy (whipping) cream
1 cup chicken or vegetable broth
2 tablespoons butter
1 cup broccoli florets, finely chopped
Ground black pepper and salt to taste
1 cup shredded cheddar cheese, plus more to garnish

Directions
1. To a skillet or saucepan, add the butter and heat it over medium heat.
2. Add the broccoli and stir-cook to sauté for about 4–5 minutes or until softened.
3. Add the cream and broth, stirring constantly. Season with salt and black pepper.
4. Cook, stirring occasionally, for 10–15 minutes, until the mixture has thickened.
5. Reduce the heat to low and simmer the mixture.
6. Add the shredded cheese and stir the mixture until the cheese dissolves.
7. Serve warm with more cheese on top.

Nutrition (per serving)
Calories 356, fat 31g, carbs 8g, protein 12g, sodium 616mg

Sausage Kale Soup

Serves 6 | Prep. time 5 minutes | Cooking time 30 minutes | $$

Ingredients
1½ quarts low-sodium chicken broth
1 large head kale, stemmed and chopped
1 tablespoon olive oil
1 pound Italian pork sausage
3 large potatoes, peeled and chopped
1 (15-ounce) can white beans, rinsed and drained
1 tablespoon Italian seasoning

Directions
1. To a cooking pot, add the oil and heat it over medium heat.
2. Add the sausage and cook for about 8–10 minutes until no longer pink.
3. Break the sausage into small pieces.
4. Add the broth, kale and potatoes. Stir-cook for 15 minutes or until the potatoes are tender.
5. Add the beans and Italian seasoning. Stir and cook for 8–10 minutes.
6. Serve warm.

Nutrition (per serving)
Calories 487, fat 27g, carbs 31g, protein 26g, sodium 1126mg

Cream Pumpkin Soup

Serves 4 | Prep. time 5 minutes | Cooking time 30 minutes | $$

Ingredients
1 small onion, finely cut
1 large potato, peeled and chopped
1 pound pumpkin, peeled and diced
3 cups vegetable broth
¼ cup sour cream

Directions
1. Add the oil to a skillet or saucepan and heat it over medium heat.
2. Add the onion and stir-cook to sauté for about 2–3 minutes or until softened.
3. Add the vegetable broth and boil the mixture.
4. Reduce heat to medium-low.
5. Add the pumpkin and potato; simmer, stirring occasionally, for 25 minutes or until the pumpkin is cooked well.
6. Serve warm with the sour cream on top.

Nutrition (per serving)
Calories 148, fat 3g, carbs 17g, protein 3g, sodium 124mg

Tomato Cream Soup

Serves 4 | Prep. time 5 minutes | Cooking time 20 minutes | $

Ingredients
2 cloves garlic, minced
½ tablespoon dried basil
1 quart vegetable broth
2 (14½-ounce) cans fire-roasted diced tomatoes
½ cup heavy cream
Black pepper and salt to taste
2 tablespoons basil, finely chopped

Directions
1. To a skillet or saucepan, add the broth and heat it over medium heat.
2. Add the tomatoes, garlic, and dried basil; stir-cook for 5 minutes.
3. Reduce the heat to low, mix in the cream, cover with a lid, and simmer the mixture for 15 minutes.
4. Puree the mixture in a blender until smooth.
5. Season with black pepper and salt to taste.
6. Serve warm with the basil on top.

Nutrition (per serving)
Calories 164, fat 11g, carbs 13g, protein 5g, sodium 627mg

Spinach Pasta Soup

Serves 6 | Prep. time 5 minutes | Cooking time 12–15 minutes | $

Ingredients
1½ cups dried Ditalini or other small pasta
2 quarts low-sodium chicken broth
6 ounces baby spinach, chopped
3 large eggs, beaten
¼ cup Parmesan cheese, grated, plus more to serve
Black pepper and salt to taste

Directions
1. To a skillet or saucepan, add the broth and heat it over medium heat.
2. Add the spinach and pasta. Cook the pasta for about 8 minutes or until cooked well.
3. In a mixing bowl, combine the eggs and grated cheese.
4. Add the egg mixture to the soup and stir well.
5. Season with black pepper and salt to taste.
6. Serve warm with some more cheese.

Nutrition (per serving)
Calories 208, fat 7g, carbs 11g, protein 18g, sodium 628mg

Beef Veggie Soup

Serves 6 | Prep. time 5 minutes | Cooking time 90 minutes | $$

Ingredients
1½ quarts low-sodium beef broth
½–¾ cup chopped onions
1 teaspoon garlic powder or minced garlic cloves
2 tablespoons olive oil
1 pound beef top, cubed
1 (14-ounce) can diced tomatoes
4 small potatoes, peeled and chopped
Black pepper and salt to taste

Directions
1. Add the oil to a skillet or saucepan and heat it over medium heat.
2. Add the beef cubes and stir-cook for 2–3 minutes per side until evenly brown.
3. Add the broth and tomatoes; stir gently.
4. Reduce the heat to low and simmer the mixture. Cover it with a lid and cook for 55–60 minutes.
5. Add the potatoes and vegetables. Stir and cook for 15–20 minutes or until the potatoes are tender.
6. Season with black pepper and salt to taste. Serve warm.

Nutrition (per serving)
Calories 501, fat 12g, carbs 42g, protein 38g, sodium 237mg

POULTRY & CHICKEN

Cheesy Backed Chicken

Serves 6 | Prep. time 5 minutes | Cooking time 45 minutes | $$

Ingredients
1 cup breadcrumbs
½ cup milk
6 chicken breast halves
1 cup Monterrey Jack cheese, shredded
1 ounce powdered ranch dressing mix
Black pepper and salt to taste

Directions
1. Season the chicken with some black pepper and salt.
2. Preheat the oven to 350°F or 175°C. Grease a baking dish with melted butter.
3. Mix the dressing mix with cheese and breadcrumbs in a mixing bowl. Season with a pinch of black pepper and salt.
4. Coat the chicken breasts in the milk in another bowl. Then coat them with the crumb mixture.
5. Arrange over a greased baking dish.
6. Bake for 40–45 minutes. Serve warm.

Nutrition (per serving)
Calories 208, fat 6g, carbs 7g, protein 27g, sodium 264mg

Bacon Grilled Chicken

Serves 4 | Prep. time 10 minutes | Cooking time 10 minutes | $

Ingredients
4 teaspoons garlic powder
2 chicken breasts, halved
4 strips bacon
4 sprigs rosemary, chopped
Black pepper to taste

Directions
1. Preheat the grill.
2. Season the chicken breast halves with black pepper and salt.
3. Coat them with rosemary and garlic powder.
4. Wrap 1 bacon strip around each chicken breast half.
5. Secure them with a toothpick.
6. Grill for 8–10 minutes on each side, until the chicken is cooked well.
7. Serve warm.

Nutrition (per serving)
Calories 203, fat 7g, carbs 6g, protein 28g, sodium 321mg

Turkey Sausage Feast

Serves 4 | Prep. time 5 minutes | Cooking time 45 minutes | $$

Ingredients
3 cloves garlic, minced
½ cup red wine
2 tablespoons olive oil
1 pound hot Italian turkey sausage links, cut into small pieces
1 (28-ounce) can crushed tomatoes
1 tablespoon dried basil
Red pepper flakes and salt to taste

Directions
1. Add the oil to a skillet or saucepan and heat it over medium heat.
2. Add the sausage and stir-cook for 8–10 minutes until evenly brown.
3. Add the garlic and cook for 3 minutes, until fragrant.
4. Add the wine, tomatoes and basil.
5. Reduce the heat to low and simmer the mixture. Cover it with a lid and cook for 25–30 minutes.
6. Add salt and red pepper to taste. Serve warm.

Nutrition (per serving)
Calories 542, fat 28g, carbs 37g, protein 41g, sodium 954mg

Pomegranate Turkey Meal

Serves 4 | Prep. time 10 minutes | Cooking time 35 minutes | $$

Ingredients
1 cup pomegranate juice
5 teaspoons canola oil (divided)
4 turkey cutlets
4 fennel bulbs, thinly sliced
1 teaspoon cornstarch
Black pepper and salt to taste

Directions
1. Preheat the oven to 450°F or 230°C. Line a baking sheet with parchment paper.
2. Add the fennel to a mixing bowl along with 3 teaspoons of oil, a pinch of black pepper and salt.
3. Toss well and arrange over a baking sheet.
4. Roast for 25 minutes.
5. Season the turkey cutlets with some black pepper and salt.
6. To a skillet or saucepan, add the remaining oil and heat it over medium heat.
7. Add the turkey cutlets and stir-cook until evenly brown for 4–5 minutes per side.
8. Drain the cutlets and wrap them in a piece of foil. Set aside.
9. Add the pomegranate juice to the skillet or saucepan. Boil the mixture.
10. Add the cornstarch and whisk the mixture until it is completely dissolved.
11. Place the cutlets on a serving plate; top with the roasted fennel and pomegranate sauce.
12. Serve warm.

Nutrition (per serving)
Calories 184, fat 6g, carbs 23g, protein 6g, sodium 186mg

Italian Turkey Roast

Serves 6 | Prep. time 5 minutes | Cooking time 2 hours | $$

Ingredients
1 tablespoon Italian seasoning
2 teaspoons seasoned salt
1 (4–5 pound) turkey breast, skin on
1 tablespoon olive oil
½ teaspoon black pepper
1 cup vegetable broth
Cooking spray

Directions
1. Preheat the oven to 375°F or 190°C. Grease a casserole dish with cooking spray.
2. Arrange the turkey breast in the casserole dish and coat with the olive oil.
3. Rub the turkey breast with the Italian seasoning, black pepper and seasoned salt.
4. Pour the broth over it.
5. Roast for 1½–2 hours, until the turkey is cooked well.
6. Slice and serve with the juice left in the casserole dish.

Nutrition (per serving)
Calories 412, fat 14g, carbs 7g, protein 53g, sodium 957mg

Artichoke Baked Chicken

Serves 4 | Prep. time 5 min. | Cooking time 20–25 min. | $$

Ingredients
1 (14-ounce) can artichoke hearts, drained
4 chicken breast halves
1 (14½-ounce) can diced tomatoes
¼ cup tomato paste
½ tablespoon olive oil
Black pepper and salt to taste

Directions
1. Season the chicken breasts with some black pepper and salt.
2. Add the oil to a skillet or saucepan and heat it over medium heat.
3. Add the chicken breasts and stir-cook for 6–8 minutes per side until evenly brown. Set aside.
4. Add the tomato, artichoke hearts, tomato paste, and a pinch of black pepper and salt.
5. Stir-cook the mixture for 3 minutes on low heat. Return the chicken breasts and cook for 8–10 more minutes, stirring occasionally.
6. Serve warm.

Nutrition (per serving)
Calories 264, fat 6g, carbs 7g, protein 28g, sodium 428mg

Classic Lime Butter Chicken

Serves 4 | Prep. time 5 minutes | Cooking time 20 minutes | $

Ingredients
¼ cup vegetable oil
Juice of 1 lime
6 chicken breasts
½ cup butter
½ teaspoon dried basil
Black pepper and salt to taste

Directions
1. Season the chicken with some black pepper and salt.
2. Add the oil to a skillet or saucepan and heat it over medium heat.
3. Add the chicken and stir-cook for 3–4 minutes per side until evenly brown.
4. Put on the lid and cook for 8–10 min on low heat.
5. Drain the chicken and set it aside.
6. To the pan, add the lime juice and butter.
7. Heat the mixture to thicken. Mix in the basil and a pinch of salt.
8. Top the sauce over the chicken; serve warm.

Nutrition (per serving)
Calories 526, fat 23g, carbs 12g, protein 36g, sodium 332mg

Chicken Mushroom Mystery Stew

Serves 4 | Prep. time 5 minutes | Cooking time 35 minutes | $$

Ingredients
½ cup water
2 tablespoons olive oil
4 chicken breast halves
½ pound mushrooms, thinly sliced
1 tablespoon butter
Black pepper and salt to taste

Directions
1. Season the chicken breasts with some black pepper and salt.
2. Add the oil to a skillet or saucepan and heat it over medium heat.
3. Add the chicken breasts and stir-cook for 5–6 minutes per side until evenly brown.
4. Preheat the oven to 375°F or 190°C. Line a baking sheet with parchment paper.
5. Arrange the cooked chicken over a baking sheet and bake for 18–20 minutes.
6. Meanwhile, melt the butter in another skillet and sauté the mushrooms for 4–5 minutes.
7. Add the water, a pinch of black pepper and salt; stir-cook for another 2–3 minutes.
8. Add the chicken breasts and stir the mixture.
9. Serve warm.

Nutrition (per serving)
Calories 246, fat 13g, carbs 6g, protein 24g, sodium 217mg

PORK, BEEF, LAMB & VEAL

Rosemary Lamb Chops

Serves 4 | Prep. time 5 minutes | Cooking time 15 minutes | $$

Ingredients
8 lamb loin chops, about 2 pounds
1 teaspoon dried rosemary
1 teaspoon seasoned salt
½ teaspoon black pepper
2 tablespoons olive oil
¼ cup balsamic vinegar
1 tablespoon honey
1–2 tablespoons butter, melted

Directions
1. Season the lamb chops with the salt, black pepper and rosemary.
2. Add the oil to a skillet or saucepan and heat it over medium heat.
3. Add the lamb chops; stir-cook for 4–5 minutes on each side or until cooked well. Transfer to a container and cover with aluminum foil.
4. Add the vinegar and honey to the skillet or saucepan; stir the mixture.
5. Cook for 3–5 minutes on low heat to thicken the sauce.
6. Stir in the butter and mix well.
7. Return the lamb chops to the saucepan and combine well.
8. Serve warm.

Nutrition (per serving)
Calories 415, fat 18g, carbs 16g, protein 45g, sodium 421mg

Avocado Beef Salad

Serves 2 | Prep. time 5 minutes | Cooking time 10 minutes | $$

Ingredients
2 cups romaine lettuce, chopped
1 avocado, cubed
½ cup grape tomatoes, halved
1 tablespoon vegetable oil
1 pound ground beef
Ground black pepper and salt to taste
½ cup shredded cheese

Directions
1. Add the oil to a skillet or saucepan and heat it over medium heat.
2. Add the ground beef, breaking it into smaller pieces.
3. Stir-cook until the beef is evenly browned, about 8–10 minutes. Season with black pepper and salt.
4. Add the romaine lettuce into two bowls. Season with more black pepper and salt.
5. Add the avocado, tomatoes, cooked beef and shredded cheese.
6. Toss and serve fresh.

Nutrition (per serving)
Calories 586, fat 28g, carbs 12g, protein 47g, sodium 871mg

BBQ Orange Pork Chops

Serves 4 | Prep. time 10 minutes | Cooking time 20 minutes | $$

Ingredients
½ cup barbecue sauce
⅓ cup orange juice
4 thick pork rib chops
1 yellow onion, diced
3 teaspoons canola oil (divided)
Melted butter (to grease)
Black pepper and salt to taste

Directions
1. Preheat the oven to 400°F or 204°C. Grease a baking dish with melted butter.
2. Season the pork chops with some black pepper and salt.
3. To a skillet or saucepan, add 2 tablespoons of oil and heat it over medium heat.
4. Add the pork chops and stir-cook for 2 minutes per side until evenly brown. Set them aside. Heat the remaining oil; sauté the onion for 4 minutes.
5. Stir in the orange juice and cook for 1 minute.
6. Add the barbecue sauce and cooked pork chops.
7. Stir and add them to a greased baking dish.
8. Bake the pork chops for 10 minutes. Serve warm.

Nutrition (per serving)
Calories 358, fat 9g, carbs 18g, protein 23g, sodium 532mg

Seasoned Beef Tomato Meal

Serves 6 | Prep. time 5 minutes | Cooking time 45 minutes | $

Ingredients
1 tablespoon garlic, crushed or minced
1 pound lean ground beef
1 tablespoon olive oil
⅓ cup onion, finely chopped
1 tablespoon Italian seasoning
1 (28-ounce) can crushed tomatoes
½ cup red wine
Black pepper and salt to taste

Directions
1. Add the oil to a skillet or saucepan and heat it over medium heat.
2. Add the onion and stir-cook to sauté for about 5 minutes or until softened.
3. Add the garlic and sauté for another 3 minutes.
4. Add the ground beef and stir-cook for 4–5 minutes or until evenly brown.
5. Add the Italian seasoning, onion powder, tomatoes and wine. Stir well.
6. Reduce the heat to low, cover with a lid, and simmer the mixture for 25–30 minutes, until the sauce is thickened.
7. Season with black pepper and salt to taste. Serve warm.

Nutrition (per serving)
Calories 328, fat 9g, carbs 10 g, protein 17g, sodium 129mg

Veggie Sausage Pan Feast

Serves 4 | Prep. time 5 minutes | Cooking time 25 minutes | $$

Ingredients
1 large red bell pepper, seeded and cut into thin strips
4 medium potatoes, peeled and cubed
1 large onion, peeled, halved, and thinly sliced
1 tablespoon olive oil
1 teaspoon seasoned salt
5–6 Italian sausage links

Directions
1. Preheat the oven to 400°F or 204°C. Line a baking sheet with parchment paper.
2. In a mixing bowl, combine the potatoes, onion, and bell pepper.
3. Add the olive oil and sprinkle with the seasoned salt.
4. Arrange the mixture on the baking sheet and place the sausages over the vegetables.
5. Roast for about 25 minutes or until the sausages are cooked well.
6. Remove from the oven and let cool.
7. Slice the sausage links into pieces and serve with the vegetables.

Nutrition (per serving)
Calories 319, fat 13g, carbs 27g, protein 23g, sodium 1047mg

Super Salami Salad

Serves 4 | Prep. time 5 minutes | Cooking time 0 minutes | $$$

Ingredients
6 ounces cooked salami, diced
6 ounces provolone cheese, diced
½ head iceberg lettuce, quartered
1 cup grape tomatoes, halved
⅓ cup vinaigrette

Directions
1. Place the lettuce quarters in a large bowl.
2. Add the tomatoes, salami, and cheese. Drizzle the vinaigrette on top.
3. Toss well and serve fresh.

Nutrition (per serving)
Calories 286, fat 22g, carbs 7g, protein 17g, sodium 946mg

Broccoli Sausage Pasta

Serves 5–6 | Prep. time 5 minutes | Cooking time 25 minutes | $$

Ingredients
1 bunch broccoli florets
½ pound cavatelli or other pasta
¾ pound Italian sausages, sliced
½ tablespoon olive oil
2 cloves garlic, minced
Black pepper and salt to taste

Directions
1. Cook the pasta according to package directions. Drain and set aside, reserving ½ cup of the cooking water.
2. Heat some water over medium-high heat in a large cooking pot.
3. Add the broccoli and some salt. Cook for 3–4 minutes and then drain the water.
4. Add the oil to a skillet or saucepan and heat it over medium heat.
5. Add the sausage and stir-cook for 4–5 minutes per side until evenly brown.
6. Add the cooked broccoli and garlic; stir-cook for 2–3 minutes.
7. Stir in the pasta with the reserved cooking water. Season with black pepper and salt and cook for 1 minute.
8. Serve warm.

Nutrition (per serving)
Calories 517, fat 18g, carbs 41g, protein 26g, sodium 738mg

Beef Noodle Mania

Serves 4 | Prep. time 5 minutes | Cooking time 20 minutes | $$

Ingredients
½ pound egg noodles
½ cup sour cream
1 pound lean beef, minced
1 (10½-ounce) can condensed cream of mushroom soup
1 tablespoon garlic powder
Vegetable oil
Black pepper and salt to taste

Directions
1. Cook the noodles according to package directions. Drain and set aside.
2. Add the oil to a skillet or saucepan and heat it over medium heat.
3. Add the beef and stir-cook for 3–4 minutes per side until evenly brown. Drain the liquid.
4. Add the soup and garlic powder; stir and simmer for 10 minutes on low heat.
5. Add the noodles, sour cream, black pepper and salt; simmer for 2 minutes. Serve warm.

Nutrition (per serving)
Calories 389, fat 22g, carbs 18g, protein 26g, sodium 668mg

Buttery Veal Mushroom

Serves 5–6 | Prep. time 5 min. | Cooking time 15–20 min. | $$

Ingredients
¼ cup all-purpose flour
6 (4–5-ounce) veal escalopes (cutlets)
¼ cup olive oil
1 shallot, minced
½ cup red wine
2 cups vegetable or chicken stock
1 tablespoon butter (optional)
3 cups thinly sliced mushrooms, cremini or shiitake

Directions
1. Season the veal escalopes with black pepper and salt. Coat evenly with the flour and set aside.
2. Add the oil to a skillet or saucepan and heat it over medium heat.
3. Add the escalopes and stir-cook until the edges turn evenly brown. Drain and set aside.
4. To the empty skillet or saucepan, add the shallots and wine.
5. Cook for 2–3 minutes to thicken the mixture.
6. Mix in the mushrooms and stock.
7. Reduce the heat to low, cover with a lid, and simmer the mixture for 4–5 minutes, until thickened.
8. Mix in the butter and season with black pepper and salt.
9. Serve the veal escalopes with the mushroom sauce on top.

Nutrition (per serving)
Calories 478, fat 27g, carbs 26g, protein 31g, sodium 98mg

FISH & SEAFOOD

Baked Chili Salmon

Serves 4 | Prep. time 5 minutes | Cooking time 20 minutes | $

Ingredients
1 tablespoon rice vinegar
2 tablespoons soy sauce
2 tablespoons sweet chili sauce
4 salmon fillets (1¼ pounds), skin on
¼ teaspoon black pepper
½ teaspoon salt
Chopped cilantro (for garnish)

Directions
1. Preheat the oven to 375°F or 190°C. Line a baking sheet with parchment paper.
2. In a mixing bowl, combine the soy sauce, chili sauce and vinegar. Set aside.
3. Season the salmon fillets with salt and black pepper.
4. Arrange the fillets on the baking sheet. Add the sauce mixture over the salmon.
5. Bake for about 14–15 minutes or until the fish is tender and light pink.
6. Top with chopped cilantro. Serve warm.

Nutrition (per serving)
Calories 258, fat 13g, carbs 4g, protein 27g, sodium 879mg

Shrimp Mayo Salad

Serves 2–3 | Prep. time 5 minutes | Cooking time 2 minutes | $$

Ingredients
1 tablespoon olive oil
1 avocado, cubed
1 celery stalk, chopped
¼ cup mayonnaise
1 pound shrimp, peeled and deveined
Ground black pepper and Himalayan salt to taste
1 teaspoon lime juice

Directions
1. Add the oil to a skillet or saucepan and heat it over medium heat.
2. Add the shrimp; stir-cook for 1–2 minutes until they turn light pink.
3. Season with salt and black pepper.
4. Add the shrimp to a mixing bowl, cover, and refrigerate.
5. In another bowl, combine the avocado, celery, and mayonnaise.
6. Mix in the lime juice and more salt to taste.
7. Add the chilled shrimp. Toss. Serve chilled.

Nutrition (per serving)
Calories 516, fat 28g, carbs 14g, protein 51g, sodium 548mg

Classic Shrimp & Potatoes

Serves 4 | Prep. time 10 minutes | Cooking time 15 minutes | $

Ingredients
2 tablespoons olive oil (divided)
2 teaspoons curry powder
1 pound large shrimp
2 large potatoes, peeled and diced
Black pepper and salt to taste
Chopped parsley (to serve)

Directions
1. Add the shrimp to a mixing bowl along with the curry powder, salt and black pepper. Toss the mixture well.
2. Add 1 tablespoon of the oil to a skillet or saucepan and heat it over medium heat.
3. Add the shrimp and cook for 3 minutes until they turn pink.
4. Add the remaining oil to another skillet or saucepan and heat it over low heat.
5. Stir cook the potatoes for 12–14 minutes, until crisp.
6. Season with black pepper and salt. Serve the potatoes with the shrimp.
7. Top with chopped parsley.

Nutrition (per serving)
Calories 198, fat 7g, carbs 23g, protein 28g, sodium 462mg

Cheesy Baked Tilapia

Serves 4 | Prep. time 8 minutes | Cooking time 12 minutes | $

Ingredients
¾ cup Parmesan cheese, grated
4 tilapia fillets
2 tablespoons olive oil
2 teaspoons paprika
Black pepper and salt to taste

Directions
1. Preheat the oven to 400°F or 204°C. Line a baking sheet with parchment paper.
2. Coat the fish fillets with the olive oil.
3. In a mixing bowl, combine the cheese, paprika and a pinch black pepper and salt.
4. Coat the fish fillets with the cheese mixture.
5. Place the tilapia fillets on the baking sheet.
6. Bake for 10–12 min. Serve warm.

Nutrition (per serving)
Calories 398, fat 26g, carbs 4g, protein 32g, sodium 1247mg

Cajun White Wine Shrimp

Serves 5–6 | Prep. time 5 minutes | Cooking time 10 minutes | $

Ingredients
1 pound large shrimp, peeled and deveined
½ cup white wine
1 tablespoon olive oil
2 cloves garlic, crushed
1 tablespoon Cajun seasoning
1 tablespoon Italian seasoning
Lemon wedges (to serve; optional)

Directions
1. Add the oil to a skillet or saucepan and heat it over medium heat.
2. Add the garlic and shrimp; stir-cook for about 2 minutes or until the garlic turns fragrant.
3. Add the wine, Cajun and Italian seasonings; stir the mixture.
4. Stir in the shrimp; cook for about 3–4 minutes or until the shrimp turn evenly pink.
5. Serve warm.

Nutrition (per serving)
Calories 103, fat 3g, carbs 2g, protein 19g, sodium 547mg

Teriyaki Salmon Rice Meal

Serves 4 | Prep. time 5 min. | Cooking time 20–25 min. | $$

Ingredients
1 pound salmon fillets, diced
¼ cup teriyaki sauce
1 tablespoon olive oil
1¼ cups long grain rice
Black pepper and salt to taste

Directions
1. Cook the rice according to package directions. Drain and set aside.
2. Add the oil to a skillet or saucepan and heat it over medium heat.
3. Add the salmon with a pinch black pepper and salt. Stir-cook for 7–8 minutes.
4. Add the rice and teriyaki sauce. Combine and cook for another 2 minutes.
5. Serve warm.

Nutrition (per serving)
Calories 428, fat 7g, carbs 46g, protein 14g, sodium 710mg

Salmon Mustard Bake

Serves 4 | Prep. time 5 minutes | Cooking time 15 minutes | $

Ingredients
¼ cup breadcrumbs, dry
¼ cup butter, melted
4 (6-ounce) salmon fillets
3 tablespoons Dijon mustard
Black pepper and salt to taste

Directions
1. Preheat the oven to 400°F or 204°C. Line a baking sheet with parchment paper.
2. Season the salmon fillets with some black pepper and salt.
3. Arrange them on the lined baking sheet.
4. Top with the mustard and then with the breadcrumbs.
5. Drizzle the butter on top and bake for 15 minutes, until the salmon is tender.
6. Serve warm.

Nutrition (per serving)
Calories 376, fat 26g, carbs 7g, protein 34g, sodium 168mg

VEGAN & VEGETARIAN

Chickpea Spinach Salad

Serves 4–6 | Prep. time 5 minutes | Cooking time 0 minutes | $$

Ingredients
½ cup crumbled feta cheese
2 cups grape tomatoes
10–12 ounces baby spinach
1 cup canned chickpeas, drained and rinsed
⅓ cup vinaigrette

Directions
1. In a mixing bowl, combine the spinach, chickpeas, cheese and tomatoes.
2. Toss the mixture well; top with the vinaigrette.
3. You can serve the salad fresh or after chilling for 15–30 minutes in your fridge.

Nutrition (per serving)
Calories 154, fat 7g, carbs 14g, protein 7g, sodium 404mg

Arugula Cheese Salad

Serves 4 | Prep. time 5–8 minutes | Cooking time 0 minutes | $$

Ingredients
1 tablespoon honey
6 ounces arugula, chopped
3 tablespoons olive oil
2 tablespoons balsamic vinegar
2 cups sliced strawberries
⅓ cup blue cheese, crumbled
Black pepper and salt to taste

Directions
1. In a mixing bowl, combine the oil, vinegar and honey. Set aside.
2. Add the arugula to another bowl. Top with the strawberries.
3. Toss the mixture well; top with the dressing and toss again.
4. Top with the cheese, black pepper and salt.
5. You can serve the salad fresh or after chilling for 15–30 minutes in your fridge.

Nutrition (per serving)
Calories 146, fat 13g, carbs 12g, protein 3g, sodium 134mg

Tomato Couscous Salad

Serves 4 | Prep. time 5 minutes | Cooking time 0 minutes | $

Ingredients
3 tablespoons olive oil
2 tablespoons lemon juice
2 cups cooked couscous
3 ripe tomatoes, diced
1 tablespoon dried mint
Salt to taste

Directions
1. In a mixing bowl, combine the couscous and tomatoes.
2. Toss the mixture well.
3. In another bowl, combine the olive oil, lemon juice and mint.
4. Top over the salad and toss well. Season with salt to taste.
5. You can serve the salad fresh or after chilling for 15–30 minutes in your fridge.

Nutrition (per serving)
Calories 183, fat 9g, carbs 18g, protein 3g, sodium 46mg

Broccoli Cheese Pasta

Serves 6 | Prep. time 5 minutes | Cooking time 20 minutes | $

Ingredients
1 pound uncooked spaghetti
2 bunches broccoli, trimmed and cut into florets
4 cloves garlic, minced
1 teaspoon salt
2 tablespoons butter, melted
⅓ cup olive oil
Red pepper flakes to taste

Directions
1. Heat water over medium-high heat in a large cooking pot.
2. Add the spaghetti and cook for 10–12 minutes, adding the broccoli florets after 7 minutes.
3. Cook until the noodles are cooked well. Drain and set aside.
4. Add the butter to the pot and heat it over medium heat.
5. Add the olive oil. Stir in the garlic and salt.
6. Stir-cook for 2–3 minutes or until fragrant.
7. Add the cooked broccoli and spaghetti; toss the mixture well.
8. Season with red pepper to taste. Serve warm.

Nutrition (per serving)
Calories 479, fat 17g, carbs 52g, protein 16g, sodium 482mg

Tomato Bean Salad

Serves 4–5 | Prep. time 5–8 minutes | Cooking time 0 | $$

Ingredients
3 tablespoons basil, chopped
⅓ cup feta cheese, crumbled
1 (15-ounce) can white beans, drained and rinsed
1 pint grape tomatoes, halved
¼ cup vinaigrette
Black pepper to taste

Directions
1. In a mixing bowl, combine the beans, tomatoes, basil, and cheese.
2. Toss the mixture well; top with the vinaigrette. Season to taste with black pepper.
3. You can serve the salad fresh or after chilling for 15–30 minutes in your fridge.

Nutrition (per serving)
Calories 211, fat 9g, carbs 22g, protein 10 g, sodium 414mg

Classic Cheese Pizza

Serves 4 | Prep. time 10 minutes | Cooking time 30 minutes | $$

Ingredients
½ cup tomato sauce
1 store-bought pizza dough
2 cloves garlic, crushed
¾ cup herbed goat cheese, crumbled
1 cup Mozzarella cheese, chopped

Directions
1. Preheat the oven to 450°F or 230°C.
2. Roll the dough out onto a floured surface to make a 12-inch round shape.
3. Place it on a parchment-lined baking sheet or a pizza stone.
4. Top it with the tomato sauce, garlic and both the cheeses.
5. Bake for 25–30 minutes or until the crust is golden brown.
6. Slice and serve the pizza warm.

Nutrition (per serving)
Calories 428, fat 16g, carbs 8g, protein 15g, sodium 547mg

Corn Bean Chili

Serves 6 | Prep. time 5 minutes | Cooking time 25 minutes | $

Ingredients
1–2 tablespoons chili powder
1 tablespoon olive oil
1 medium yellow onion, peeled and diced
2 (14-ounce) cans diced tomatoes with green chilies
1 (10-ounce) pack frozen corn
2 (15-ounce) cans white beans, rinsed and drained
Black pepper and salt to taste

Directions
1. In a large cooking pot, heat the olive oil over medium-high heat.
2. Add the onion and stir-cook to sauté for about 5 minutes or until softened.
3. Add the chili powder, tomatoes with chili, and corn. Stir-cook for a few minutes and then add the beans.
4. Reduce the heat to low, cover with a lid, and simmer the mixture for 12–15 minutes.
5. Season with black pepper and salt to taste. Serve warm.

Nutrition (per serving)
Calories 323, fat 12g, carbs 38g, protein 14g, sodium 924mg

DESSERTS

Blueberry Cobbler Delight

Serves 8 | Prep. time 5–8 minutes | Cooking time 60 minutes | $

Ingredients
1 cup whole milk
1 cup all-purpose flour
1 quart blueberries
1 cup white sugar
1½ teaspoons baking powder
½ teaspoon salt
½ cup butter, melted

Directions
1. Preheat the oven to 350°F or 175°C. Grease a baking dish with melted butter.
2. In a mixing bowl, combine the flour, salt and baking powder.
3. Add the milk and sugar to the bowl and combine until smooth.
4. Add the blueberries.
5. Pour the batter into the greased baking dish.
6. Bake the cobbler for 60 minutes or until the top is golden brown.
7. Cool down for a while, slice and serve.

Nutrition (per serving)
Calories 315, fat 15g, carbs 35g, protein 7g, sodium 246mg

Cream Lime Pie

Serves 6 | Prep. time 10 minutes | Cooking time 15 minutes | $

Ingredients
1 (6-ounce) baked graham cracker crust
1 (14-ounce) can condensed milk, sweetened
3 egg yolks
½ cup lime juice
1 cup whipped cream

Directions
1. Preheat the oven to 350°F or 175°C.
2. To a mixing bowl, add the condensed milk, egg yolks, and lime juice. Whisk the mixture well.
3. Add the mixture into the cracker crust. Bake for 10–12 minutes or until golden brown.
4. Take out and cool down for 15 minutes.
5. Chill in the refrigerator for 3–4 hours.
6. Top with whipped cream and serve chilled.

Nutrition (per serving)
Calories 542, fat 28g, carbs 52g, protein 9g, sodium 218mg

Apple Cinnamon Pudding

Serves 8 | Prep. time 15 minutes | Cooking time 50 minutes | $$

Ingredients
1 teaspoon cinnamon
3 eggs, beaten
8 slices white bread, cubed
2 cups half-and-half cream
½ cup + 2 tablespoons sugar (divided)
2 apples, peeled, cored and chopped
Cooking spray

Directions
1. Preheat the oven to 350°F or 175°C. Coat an 8-inch square baking dish with cooking spray.
2. To a mixing bowl, add the half-and-half, ½ cup sugar, cinnamon and eggs. Whisk well.
3. Add the bread cubes and apples to the baking dish and mix well.
4. Add the cream mixture over the top. Set aside for 5 minutes.
5. Bake for 30 minutes.
6. Take out the dish and sprinkle the remaining sugar on top.
7. Bake for 20–25 minutes more or until the top is golden brown.
8. Cool down for a while, divide into portions and serve warm.

Nutrition (per serving)
Calories 223, fat 9g, carbs 31g, protein 6g, sodium 138mg

RECIPE INDEX

ALSO BY LOUISE DAVIDSON

Here are some of Louise Davidson's other cookbooks.

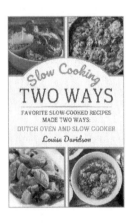

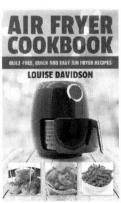

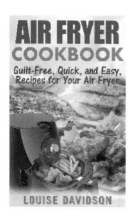

APPENDIX

Cooking Conversion Charts

1. Measuring Equivalent Chart

Type	Imperial	Imperial	Metric
Weight	1 dry ounce		28g
	1 pound	16 dry ounces	0.45 kg
Volume	1 teaspoon		5 ml
	1 dessert spoon	2 teaspoons	10 ml
	1 tablespoon	3 teaspoons	15 ml
	1 Australian tablespoon	4 teaspoons	20 ml
	1 fluid ounce	2 tablespoons	30 ml
	1 cup	16 tablespoons	240 ml
	1 cup	8 fluid ounces	240 ml
	1 pint	2 cups	470 ml
	1 quart	2 pints	0.95 l
	1 gallon	4 quarts	3.8 l
Length	1 inch		2.54 cm

* Numbers are rounded to the closest equivalent

2. Oven Temperature Equivalent Chart

Fahrenheit (°F)	Celsius (°C)	Gas Mark
220	100	
225	110	1/4
250	120	1/2
275	140	1
300	150	2
325	160	3
350	180	4
375	190	5
400	200	6
425	220	7
450	230	8
475	250	9
500	260	

* Celsius (°C) = T (°F)-32] * 5/9

** Fahrenheit (°F) = T (°C) * 9/5 + 32

*** Numbers are rounded to the closest equivalent

Made in United States
Orlando, FL
14 October 2023